THINK FACTORY: SOLAR SYSTEM

BY MELVIN AND GILDA BERGER

For Ben, Salt of the Earth, B & Z

CONTENTS

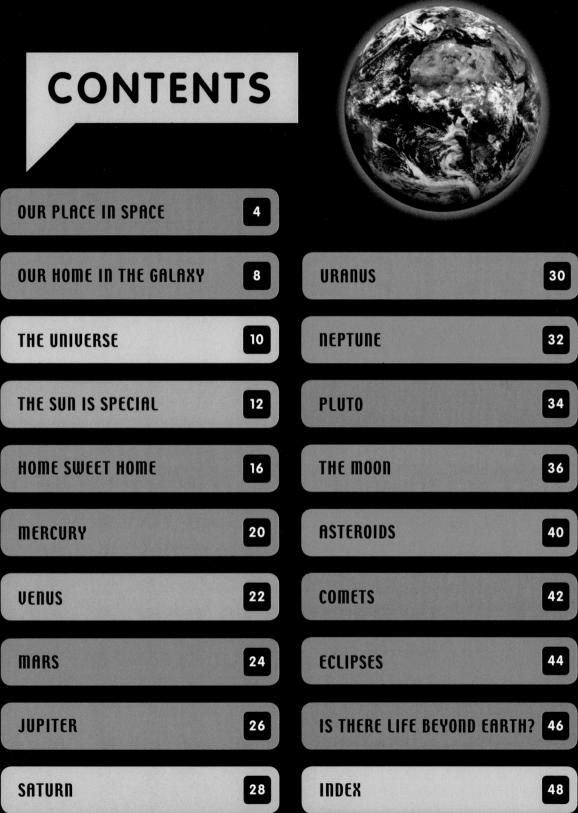

OUR PLACE IN SPACE

WHERE WE LIVE

Your address is the number of your house, the street you live on, your city, state, and country. But here's some food for thought: Your country is only one country on planet Earth. Earth is only one planet among nine that travel around the sun in the solar system. The solar system is only one part of a galaxy of stars and planets called the Milky Way. And the Milky Way is only one of billions of galaxies that make up the universe!

THE SOLAR SYSTEM

The sun is a star at the center of our solar system. Nine big bodies, called planets, travel around the sun in a counterclockwise (clock running backward) direction. Starting from the sun, the nine planets of the solar system are Mercury, Venus, Earth, Mars, Jupiter, Saturn, Uranus, Neptune, and Pluto. The planets in order have the same first letters as the words of this sentence: **M**y **V**ery **E**ducated **M**other **J**ust **S**ent **U**s **N**ine **P**izzas.

HANGING TOGETHER

Gravity is a powerful natural force in the universe. It attracts, or pulls, all objects to one another. It keeps the various bodies in the solar system from flying off into space. The sun's gravity pulls on the planets and keeps them in their orbits. The planets' gravity pulls on the moons and keeps them moving around their planets. Gravity keeps the entire solar system from spinning out of control.

SUN

MERCURY

VENUS

EARTH

URANUS

NEPTUNE

PLUTO

SATURN

JUPITER

HUGE SIZE

Everything about the solar system is enormous. It is about 3.6 billion miles (5.8 billion km) from the sun to the edge of the solar system. Light, moving at 186,000 miles a second (300,000 kps), takes about five hours to reach Pluto, the farthest planet from the sun.

AROUND AND AROUND WE GO

The planets move in orbits, or paths, around the sun. But the solar system also contains many other smaller objects, called asteroids. Most orbit around the sun between Mars and Jupiter. Also, dozens of moons—some bigger, some smaller than our moon—are in orbit around other planets.

OUR HOME IN THE GALAXY

THE MILKY WAY

Look up at the sky on a dark, clear night and you will see what looks like a bright band of light stretching across the sky. People long ago thought the band looked like poured milk spilled among the stars. They called it the "Milky Way"—and so do we. Today we know that the band of light in the sky comes from the glow of billions of stars.

UP, UP, AND AWAY

The solar system is our home in the Milky Way galaxy. But the solar system is only a very small part of this vast neighborhood in space. The Milky Way also includes billions of other stars besides our sun. Huge numbers of planets, smaller objects, dust, and gas also belong to our galaxy.

FOR GOOD MEASURE

As you know, the Milky Way, and all galaxies, are enormous in size. Astronomers tell us the Milky Way is about 100,000 light-years from side to side. A light-year is the distance that light travels in one year. It equals 5.9 trillion miles (9.5 trillion km).

THE MILKY WAY GALAXY

The Milky Way galaxy, as seen from above, looks like a giant pinwheel, with long, curved arms. Our solar system is located in one of the arms. It is about halfway between the center of the galaxy and the outer edge.

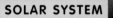
SOLAR SYSTEM

AROUND AND AROUND

The planets revolve around the sun. At the same time, the whole solar system revolves around the center of the galaxy. The solar system speeds along at about 135 miles per second (217 kps). It takes 225 million years to make one huge loop around the center of the Milky Way.

THE UNIVERSE

BIGGER THAN BIG

The universe is the very biggest thing you can imagine. It is made up of everything that exists anywhere—solar systems, stars, galaxies, and everything in, on, or in-between. But no one is sure of the actual size of the universe. Some say it has no end and goes on forever and ever. Astronomers can see out no more than about 14 billion light years.

BODY	SIZE ACROSS	
Sun	864,970 miles	(1,392,000 km)
Mercury	3,031 miles	(4,880 km)
Venus	7,520 miles	(12,102 km)
Earth	7,926 miles	(12,756 km)
Earth's Moon	2,160 miles	(3,476 km)
Mars	4,220 miles	(6,794 km)
Jupiter	88,849 miles	(142,984 km)
Saturn	74,900 miles	(120,536 km)
Uranus	31,022 miles	(49,946 km)
Neptune	30,236 miles	(48,680 km)
Pluto	1,416 miles	(2,280 km)

Distance from New York, NY, to Los Angeles, CA:
2,458 miles (3,954 km)

WHAT'S THE BIG BANG?

Most astronomers believe that the universe was born in a huge explosion called the Big Bang. They say that between 14 to 20 billion years ago, everything in the universe was scrunched tightly together in one tiny speck. Then, suddenly, the speck exploded and everything shot out in all directions. Over billions of years the bits of matter formed the galaxies, stars, and planets that make up the universe.

THE GROWING UNIVERSE

Since the Big Bang, the universe has been growing bigger and bigger. Astronomers see galaxies moving farther apart and farther away from Earth. Some say that they are still spreading out because of the energy of the Big Bang. No one knows what will happen in the future. Will the universe keep growing bigger? Or will everything in the universe come together and explode in another Big Bang?

EMPTY SPACE

Despite the enormous number of bodies in the universe, it is almost all empty space. Imagine that the universe is a box 20 miles (32 km) long, 20 miles (32 km) wide, and 20 miles (32 km) tall. Then all the stars and planets would fit into a single grain of sand inside the box. The rest of the box would be empty!

THE SUN IS SPECIAL

BIGGEST BODY

The sun is the biggest body in the solar system. Its diameter is more than 100 times bigger than the diameter of Earth. About one million planets the size of Earth could fit inside! If you drew the sun the size of a quarter, the earth would be the size of a period at the end of this sentence.

JUST ONE STEP

The average distance between the earth and the sun is about 93 million miles (150 million km). Imagine that you had a pair of magical boots. With them, each giant step would cover 93 million miles (150 million km). It would take just one step to get from Earth to the sun. But you would need another 300,000 steps to get to the next nearest star!

GREAT ENERGY

The sun is a star. Like other stars, the sun is made up mostly of two gases, hydrogen and helium. Tremendous heat and pressure inside the sun change the hydrogen into helium. This produces huge amounts of energy. From Earth, we can feel the sun's heat energy and see its light energy. The other stars are much, much farther out in space. We cannot feel their heat and we see their light only as tiny points in the night sky.

THE LIGHT FANTASTIC

Each square inch (6.4 cm^2) of the sun's surface gives off as much light as 1.5 million candles. To equal the total light that we get from the sun, we would need all the lit candles that would fit on a birthday cake 600 million miles (965 km) across!

CALL IT A YEAR

The planets of our solar system revolve in orbits around the sun. The time it takes to complete an orbit is one year on that planet. The length of the year depends on the length of the orbit and the planet's speed. Mercury is closest to the sun. It has the shortest orbit and the fastest speed. A year on Mercury lasts only 88 days. Earth is the third planet from the sun. A year on Earth is 365 days. Pluto—the farthest planet—takes about 90,000 days to complete its orbit.

PLANET	TIME IT TAKES TO ORBIT SUN
Mercury	88 Days
Venus	225 Days
Earth	365 Days
Mars	687 Days
Jupiter	12 Years
Saturn	30 Years
Uranus	84 Years
Neptune	164 Years
Pluto	248 Years

CLOSEST STAR

The sun is an ordinary star. It is not the biggest star in the universe. Yet the sun looks huge to us. That's because it is so much closer to Earth than all the other stars. And the closer an object is, the larger it looks. Since the other stars are far beyond the sun in space, they look like tiny points of light—even through powerful telescopes.

YOU ARE MY SUNSHINE

Astronomers believe the sun came into being 4.5 to 5 billion years ago. It formed, like all other stars, when gravity pulled together gases and bits of dust in space. The sun's energy comes from reactions near its center that change hydrogen into helium. This will probably go on for at least another 5 billion years. Then the sun will begin to grow larger in size and lose its heat. After billions of years more, the sun's light will finally go out.

SEEING SPOTS

If you look at a photo of the sun, you may see some dark spots on the surface. They are called sunspots. Sunspots are much cooler than the rest of the sun's surface. Most are just a few hundred miles (kilometers) across.

HOME SWEET HOME

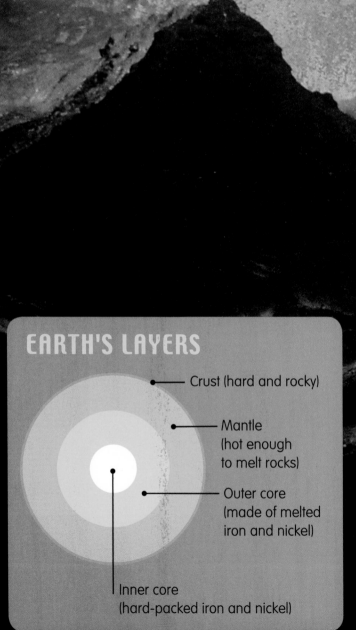

Earth was born about 4.6 billion years ago. Gravity pulled huge clouds of dust and gas together into a giant ball to form our planet. The earth, at first, was very hot. Over millions of years, it slowly cooled and became cold and dark. The sun was Earth's only source of heat and light.

EARTH'S LAYERS

Crust (hard and rocky)

Mantle (hot enough to melt rocks)

Outer core (made of melted iron and nickel)

Inner core (hard-packed iron and nickel)

UPPER CRUST

As the earth cooled, it formed a thin, hard crust of rock. Over millions of years, rain and wind slowly broke the rock down into grains of sand. Dead and decaying plants and animals mixed in with the sand. The sand became soil in which plants could grow. The earth's crust is always changing. Sometimes it happens very quickly, as when a volcano erupts. More often it happens slowly, as when mountains wear away.

POLES AND EQUATOR

The earth rotates around an imaginary line that runs through the earth. This line is called an axis. It goes from the North Pole on top to the South Pole on the bottom. Another imaginary line circles the earth around its middle. This line is called the equator. It is like a giant belt that divides the earth in half. Above the equator is the Northern Hemisphere. Below the equator is the Southern Hemisphere.

NO PLACE LIKE HOME

Earth is the only planet in the solar system with—

- temperatures that make life possible.
- an atmosphere that protects us from the sun's dangerous rays.
- gases that living beings need to breathe.
- enough water for life.

UP IN THE AIR

A layer of air covers the earth like a blanket. It is called the atmosphere. Most weather, including wind, storms, and clouds, is found in the bottom 10 miles (16 km) of the atmosphere. Big jet planes usually fly above this level. The higher you go in the atmosphere, the thinner the air. About 1,000 miles (1,600 km) above the earth, the atmosphere gradually fades into airless outer space.

DAY AND NIGHT

As the earth revolves around the sun, it also spins around, or rotates. The planet turns like a giant merry-go-round. Each complete turn takes 24 hours, or one day. When your part of Earth turns toward the sun, the sun seems to rise. It is day. The earth continues to turn until your part of Earth turns away from the sun. The sun seems to set. It is night. Sunrise, sunset. It's all in the eye of the beholder.

AROUND AND AROUND WE GO

The earth travels, or revolves, around the sun. It takes Earth one year (365 days) to finish its trip. The earth revolves at the amazing speed of nearly 70,000 miles per hour (112,620 kph). This is more than 10 times faster than a bullet. The reason you don't feel Earth moving is because everything on or near Earth, including the atmosphere, is moving with us.

REASON FOR SEASONS

The reason for seasons is the tilt of the earth. Half the year the top part of Earth, or the Northern Hemisphere, tilts toward the sun. It is spring and summer on that part of the earth and fall and winter elsewhere. The rest of the year the top part of Earth tilts away from the sun. It is fall and winter in the Northern Hemisphere and spring and summer in the Southern Hemisphere.

MERCURY THE SPEEDY PLANET

SHORT YEARS, LONG DAYS

Mercury zips around the sun faster than any other planet—about 30 miles a second (48 kps). Therefore, it takes Mercury only 88 Earth days to complete the journey, compared to 365 days for planet Earth. At the same time, Mercury rotates very, very slowly. It takes a full 59 Earth days for Mercury to spin around one time on its axis.

CLOSEST TO THE SUN

Mercury is a small, rocky planet. It is the closest planet to the sun. From Mercury, the sun looks almost three times as big as it does from Earth. In 1974, the spacecraft *Mariner 10* came within a few hundred miles (km) of Mercury and photographed half the planet.

THIN AIR

There is almost no atmosphere around Mercury. Winds do not blow and there are no storms. The thin atmosphere also allows tremendous numbe of bodies from space to crash into this small pla Over the years, these "visitors" from space have made many holes, or craters, on the planet's su Without weather, the craters remain in place for

HOT DAYS, COLD NIGHTS

By day, Mercury is hotter than a pizza oven. But at night, the temperature drops more than 1,000° Fahrenheit (600° C). That's because the thin atmosphere around Mercury does not hold in the sun's heat.

VENUS THE EARTH'S TWIN

CLOSEST NEIGHBOR

People sometimes refer to Venus as Earth's "twin." That's because Venus and Earth are both rocky planets and nearly the same size. Also, Venus is our closest neighbor in the solar system. But Venus and Earth are very different too. Venus's surface is quite hot and dry. There is no water anywhere. The atmosphere is heavy and poisonous. Earth's plants and animals could not live on Venus.

FACE-TO-FACE

When people saw Venus's stunning bright yellow color they named the planet after the Roman goddess of love and beauty. From Earth, Venus is the second brightest object in the night sky. Only the moon is brighter. Because Venus is often visible early in the evening, some call it the evening star—even though it is a planet.

PRESSURE COOKER

The clouds around Venus are very, very heavy. They press down with great weight on the surface. The pressure is 90 times the pressure on Earth's surface. So don't even think of going to Venus. The pressure would crush you as flat as a pancake!

SIZZLING SURFACE

Venus is the hottest planet in the solar system. The surface is hot enough to melt metal. The planet's great heat comes from its closeness to the sun. But the heat is also due to the planet's cloud cover. The clouds are like a thick blanket that keeps the heat in and makes the surface sizzle.

MARS THE RED PLANET

RUSTY AND DUSTY

Mars is the fourth planet from the sun. It is the only red planet. The color comes from the iron in its soil that has rusted. In fact, the soil on Mars contains twice as much iron as the soil on Earth. Powerful dust storms on Mars also blow giant clouds of soil up into the atmosphere. The flying red dust adds to Mars's red color.

A BIG MISTAKE

In 1877, Italian astronomer Giovanni Schiaparelli saw a series of lines on Mars. He called them *canali*, the Italian word for channels. By mistake, the word was translated into English as "canals." This led many people to think that the lines were canals dug by living beings on Mars. We now know that Mars has no canals and we've not been able to find any signs of intelligent life.

ON THE DOUBLE

Two small moons travel around Mars. They were discovered by astronomer Asaph Hall in 1877. He named them Phobos and Deimos, after the two sons of the god Mars. Each of Mars's moons is much smaller than our moon. Also, the moons of Mars are not round, but potato-shaped, and very fast moving. Phobos orbits Mars three times a day. Deimos takes just over a day (30 hours) for each orbit.

LANDING ON MARS

In 2004, the United States landed two spacecraft on Mars. Scientists were looking for signs of water, which is necessary for life. They found that there had been liquid water on Mars long ago. The questions they ask are: Was there life on Mars? Is there any life on Mars today? Scientists still don't have the final answers.

JUPITER THE GIANT PLANET

EUROPA

KING-SIZED

Jupiter is the biggest planet in the solar system. No wonder ancient astronomers named it after Jupiter, king of the Roman gods. More than 1,000 planets the size of Earth could fit inside Jupiter. A tunnel through Jupiter would be eleven times longer than a tunnel through Earth. A trip around Jupiter's equator would take six times longer than a trip around the earth's equator.

MADE OF GASES

Jupiter is the fifth planet from the sun. But it is the first planet that is made of gases and liquid. The four inner planets, Mercury, Venus, Earth, and Mars, are solid bodies, made of rock and metal. Jupiter, which is more like the sun, consists mainly of hydrogen.

CALLISTO

SPEED DEMON

Jupiter rotates faster than any other planet. It makes a complete rotation in less than 10 hours. If you could stand on Jupiter's equator, you would whiz around at almost 28,000 miles an hour (45,000 kph)! The fast rotation forms Jupiter's clouds into orange-and-white stripes. The high speed also makes Jupiter bulge in the middle. The planet is squashed on top and bottom.

JUPITER

IO

HIGH SPOT

The Great Red Spot is the most thrilling sight on the surface of Jupiter. The "spot" is twice as wide as the planet Earth! Most astronomers think that the Great Red Spot is a huge storm that has been raging for at least 300 years. (That's as long as people have been observing the planet.)

JUPITER'S MOONS

Jupiter has at least 62 moons. Four of the moons—Ganymede, Callisto, Io, and Europa—are very large. The largest is Ganymede. Callisto is next in size and the farthest from Jupiter. Io is smaller, and is about as big as Earth's moon. The smallest, Europa, is covered by a layer of ice many miles thick.

GANYMEDE

SATURN THE BEAUTIFUL

RINGLEADER

People know Saturn best for its bright, shiny rings. These rings are made of chunks of ice, rock, and dust. The chunks vary from tiny specks to lumps as big as automobiles. Each piece is like a mirror that reflects the sun's light. This makes the rings shine brightly.

PLANET	NUMBER OF RINGS
Mercury	0
Venus	0
Earth	0
Mars	0
Jupiter	3
Saturn	1,000s
Uranus	11
Neptune	6
Pluto	0

SECOND BIGGEST

Saturn is the second biggest planet in the solar system. Only Jupiter is bigger. Like Jupiter, Saturn is a giant gas planet that rotates very fast. It takes Saturn 30 Earth years to complete one orbit, compared to 12 years for Jupiter.
A year on Saturn is about 18 Earth years longer than a year on Jupiter.

FLOATABLE

Imagine the biggest bathtub possible. Now think of placing all the planets of the solar system into the tub, one at a time. Each planet, except for Saturn, sinks to the bottom. Saturn is so light that it floats.

HOTTER THAN YOU THINK

Saturn is the sixth planet from the sun. At that distance, it gets little of the sun's heat. Yet Saturn is not ice-cold. It produces lots of its own heat. Astronomers believe the heat comes from the gases inside Saturn. Saturn actually gives off more than twice as much heat as it gets from the sun.

MANY MOONS

Saturn has at least 37 moons. Titan is Saturn's largest moon. It is bigger than the moon that circles Earth and even bigger than the planet Mercury.

URANUS THE SIDEWAYS PLANET

SEVENTH FROM THE SUN

Uranus is the seventh planet from the sun and the third giant gas planet. It rotates like all planets. But Uranus tilts far to one side. Instead of rotating in an upright position, Uranus rolls along like a bowling ball. Uranus also travels very slowly. It takes 84 Earth years to complete one orbit.

PLANET	NUMBER OF MOONS
Mercury	0
Venus	0
Earth	1
Mars	2
Jupiter	62
Saturn	37
Uranus	27
Neptune	13
Pluto	1

SEEING THE LIGHT

Ancient people saw a tiny spot in the night sky that they thought was a star. Then, in 1781, Sir William Herschel looked at the object through a telescope. He decided it was a planet and named it Uranus after the Greek god of the sky. It was the first planet found with the help of a telescope.

MOONS AND RINGS

Uranus has many moons. Astronomers found five between 1787 and 1948 and 22 more from 1948 to today. With improved telescopes and new space shots, they may turn up others in the years to come. Uranus also has rings like the other gas giants. Its rings are mostly formed of rock, with little ice or dust.

DAY AND NIGHT

For half of its long orbit (42 years), one part of Uranus is light and the other part is dark. For the other half of its orbit (the next 42 years), the light part is dark and the dark part is light.

SPACE PROBE

The first spacecraft to fly close to Uranus was *Voyager 2*. In 1986 it passed within 50,600 miles (81,500 km) of the planet. The craft sent back many excellent pictures of Uranus's rings, moons, and blue-green color.

NEPTUNE THE LAST GAS GIANT

DOUBLE CROSS

Neptune is the eighth planet from the sun. Its orbit is between Uranus and Pluto. But every 248 years, Pluto crosses inside Neptune's orbit, making Neptune the ninth planet. For the next 20 years, Neptune is the last planet in the solar system. When Pluto crosses back, Neptune is again the eighth planet. The last crossover occurred from 1979 to 1999. It will happen next in September 2226.

CURIOUS AND CURIOUSER

Astronomers discovered Neptune in a curious way. They believed that Uranus was being pulled off course by the gravity of another planet. In searching for this mystery planet, they found Neptune in 1846. They named the planet for the Roman god of the sea.

FAR-OUT PLANET

Neptune is far beyond Uranus in the solar system. It is surrounded by thick blue clouds and is always freezing cold. Winds whip the clouds around at speeds as high as 1,200 miles per hour (1,931 kph). No one will ever walk on the surface of this planet because Neptune is mostly gas.

CONTRARY MOTION

Neptune has 13 known moons. Triton is the biggest one. Yet Triton is unlike any other large moon in the solar system. Triton orbits from east to west while all others move from west to east. Triton is also the coldest object in the solar system.

THE GREAT DARK SPOT

Photographs of Neptune show a large black area that appears and disappears. Astronomers call it the Great Dark Spot. It is a place with raging storms and great masses of swirling gases. The Great Dark Spot covers a region the size of Earth. The Great Dark Spot is similar to the Great Red Spot on Jupiter.

FARTHEST FROM THE SUN

Pluto is smaller and farther from the sun than any other planet. Yet it is not a ball of gas like Jupiter, Saturn, Uranus, and Neptune. Nor is it solid and rocky like the smaller inner planets. Instead, Pluto is mainly made of ice and rock. Some astronomers say that Pluto is not a planet at all but a comet or an asteroid.

CHARON

OOPS!

Astronomers once believed that there was a shift in the orbits of Neptune and Uranus. They thought it was due to the gravity of an unknown planet. While searching for this body, scientists found a new planet, which they named Pluto. Later, they learned that there had been no shift. But they had discovered the ninth planet.

PLUTO

LONG JOURNEY

Pluto's trip around the sun is the longest of any planet in the solar system. Also, its path is more oval-shaped. Its orbit is almost twice as long from end to end as it is from side to side. Due to its large oval orbit, Pluto crosses Neptune's orbit every 248 years. Then, Pluto becomes the eighth, instead of ninth, planet for the next 20 years.

DEEP, DEEP SPACE

Pluto is at the very edge of the solar system. It is more than 30 times farther from the sun than Earth. A spacecraft speeding from Earth at 45,000 miles per hour (72,000 kph) would need more than 9 years to get to Pluto.

GIANT MOON

Pluto has only one moon. It is called Charon. Charon is more than half the size of the planet. It is also about 20 times closer to Pluto than our moon is to Earth. Charon takes six Earth days to go around Pluto. And Pluto takes six Earth days to rotate one time. Therefore, Charon always stays in the same place in Pluto's sky. The moon never seems to rise or set.

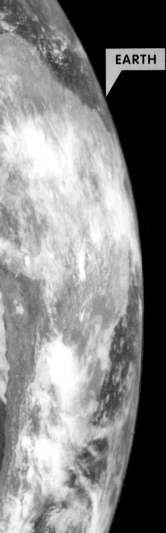

EARTH

BY THE LIGHT OF THE MOON

The moon is the brightest object in Earth's night sky. A full moon on a clear night gives enough light for you to read a book outdoors. Yet the moon does not make its own light. All of the moon's light comes from the sun. Sometimes you can see a faint outline of the moon when part of the moon is dark. That's because light from the sun bounces off Earth and casts a weak glow on the moon.

BALL OF ROCK

A moon is a ball of rock in orbit around a planet. Besides Earth's moon, there are about 140 other moons circling planets in the solar system. All moons are smaller than the planets they travel around.

CHANGING FACE

As the moon travels around Earth, it seems to change its shape. It is just over 29 days from new moon to full moon and back to new moon.

EARTH

MOON

DRY AS DUST

When Galileo first looked at the moon through a telescope, he saw many dark areas. He thought they were bodies of water and called them *Maria*, meaning "seas." Scientists later discovered that the *Maria* were really flat dry plains covered with dark lava from volcanoes.

MAN IN THE MOON

All through history, people have looked up at the moon and have seen a face on its surface. Even Abraham Lincoln once said that he saw the man in the moon. The "face" we imagine that we see is formed by the dark and light areas on the moon's surface.

THE FAR SIDE

We cannot see the far side of the moon from Earth. But photos taken by passing spacecraft show a much rougher surface than is found on the near side. The far side has many more craters, or big holes, made by lumps of rock and iron that have crashed into the moon.

MOONSCAPES

The moon is the first object in space to be visited by people from Earth. The astronauts found no life on its rocky surface. The moon has no air, no wind, and no water. Without weather, the surface has stayed the same for billions of years. At night, the moon is colder than any place on Earth. During the day, the surface is hotter than boiling water.

ASTRONAUTS ON THE MOON

An astronaut who weighs 180 pounds (81.8 kg) on Earth weighs only 30 pounds (13.6 kg) on the moon. On July 20, 1969, Neil Armstrong became the first person to walk on the moon. Over the next years, eleven other astronauts followed in his footsteps. They drove around the moon and collected rocks to bring back to Earth. Instruments they left on the moon tell us that the moon is often rocked by moonquakes, which are like weak earthquakes.

IN NAME ONLY

The word asteroid means "like a star." Yet asteroids are not stars at all. They are pieces of rock and metal, much like little planets. The largest asteroid is Ceres. It is about half the size of Pluto, the smallest planet. Big asteroids such as Ceres are round like planets. Small asteroids can be the size of giant potatoes.

ASTEROID BELT

Asteroids are found throughout the solar system. But most are grouped together in the space between Mars and Jupiter. This region is called the Asteroid Belt. Thus far, astronomers know the orbits of around 4,000 asteroids. They have photos of about 30,000 more. Some guess that about 100,000 asteroids remain to be discovered.

PLANETS AND ASTEROIDS

The planets in our solar system formed about 4.6 billion years ago. They were made up of dust and gas in orbit around the sun. Some bits of dust and gas were left over. Over millions and billions of years, gravity pulled these bits together to form the much smaller asteroids.

PULLING POWER

As the asteroids revolve around the sun, gravity from Jupiter and other large planets pulls on their orbits. This slowly moves the asteroids into new orbits. The new orbit of one small asteroid, Icarus, takes it very close to the sun. In fact, this asteroid now glows red-hot from the sun's heat. Icarus is the only asteroid near enough to see without a telescope.

THE LAST OF THE DINOSAURS

Once in a great while, an asteroid falls out of orbit and heads toward Earth. Usually it burns up before it lands. About 65 million years ago, an asteroid or comet, perhaps 9 miles (14.5 km) wide, fell in Mexico. The force of the crash sent thick clouds of dust, soil, ash, and hot steam over the entire Earth. Some scientists think it led to the extinction of many plants and animals—including the dinosaurs.

COMETS BALLS OF DIRTY ICE

TAIL ENDS

Comets are large balls of ice with gas, rocks, and dust frozen inside. There may be as many as 100 billion comets in orbit around the sun. A number of comets pass very close to the sun. The sun's heat melts some of the ice. A stream of gases and dust blows out from the comet and forms a long, shiny tail.

OUT OF SIGHT

Most comets have never been seen. They orbit the sun at the very edge of the solar system. Each of these orbits takes hundreds or thousands of years. Other comets orbit closer to the sun. Some are very bright and have very long tails. You can see them with your eyes alone. For the others, you need a telescope.

COMET CRASH

Astronomers have never seen a comet crash into Earth. But they did see a comet strike the planet Jupiter on July 16 to 22, 1994! The comet hit the planet on its far side. Light from the powerful blast was visible from Earth.

TAIL FIRST

The tail is the largest part of the comet. It forms only when the comet is near the sun. Some tails stretch over 100 million miles (160 million km) or more across the sky. All tails face away from the sun. Going toward the sun, the tail is behind the comet. But, going away from the sun, pressure from the sun pushes the tail in front of the comet!

ONCE UPON A TIME

People on Earth see Halley's Comet just about every 76 years. It is named after Edmund Halley, who saw it in 1682 and correctly predicted its return in 1758. Mark Twain was born in 1835 when Halley's Comet appeared. He died in 1910, the year Halley's Comet came back. The last time this comet came close to the earth was in 1986. It will next be seen in 2061.

SHADOW SHOWS

An eclipse is the brief blotting out of the light of an object in space. You see two kinds of eclipses from Earth. A solar eclipse occurs when the moon comes between the earth and the sun and blocks the sun's light from reaching Earth. A lunar eclipse occurs when the earth comes between the moon and the sun, blocking the sun's light from shining on the moon.

DAY INTO NIGHT

The sun is 400 times bigger than the moon. But the sun is also 400 times farther away from Earth. This makes the sun and moon look the same size in the sky. For this reason, the moon can blot out all of the sun's light when it comes between the sun and the earth. For a few minutes, day turns into night.

OUT LIKE A LIGHT

All of the moon's light comes from the sun. When Earth travels between the sun and the moon, it makes a dark shadow on the moon. The sun's light cannot reach the moon. All or part of the moon seems to disappear.

SOLAR ECLIPSE

Strange things occur during a solar eclipse. Birds stop singing. Insects stop moving. And many animals crawl into their underground homes. Some people have been known to scream when the sun disappears.

PREDICTING ECLIPSES

Astronomers have long been able to predict eclipses. When Christopher Columbus landed on the island of Jamaica, the natives refused to trade with him. Knowing that a lunar eclipse was coming, Columbus threatened to shut off the moon's light unless the islanders sold him food. As the moon grew dark, the Jamaicans quickly struck a deal.

IS THERE LIFE BEYOND EARTH?

THE SEARCH IS ON

Since 1959, astronomers have used special telescopes to search for life beyond Earth. These telescopes pick up natural radio waves from stars and other bodies in space. To find life, the astronomers listen for unusual radio signals that might be sent by intelligent beings beyond Earth. Thus far, no uncommon radio waves or signals have been received from outer space.

YOU BET!

Our Milky Way galaxy is home to billions of stars. Astronomers guess that perhaps half the stars have solar systems. They also know that the chemicals needed for life are found throughout the universe. The odds, they say, are quite good for life beyond our solar system.

SOMETHING POSSIBLE

In 1995, astronomers discovered a planet in orbit around a star much like our sun. This was the first planet ever found outside our solar system. Since then scientists have located more than 100 planets near other stars. In 1999, they discovered another entire solar system.

SPACE TRIP

One of the next space missions may be a manned trip to Mars. Getting there from Earth will be far more difficult than getting to the moon. Mars is over 200 times farther away and the trip will take about 11 months. Astronauts will need food, water, heat, and oxygen to survive. Scientists are studying ways to make life on Mars possible. Stay tuned. The Mars mission may happen in your lifetime!

UFO

Thousands of people claim to have seen UFOs (Unidentified Flying Objects or flying saucers). The United States government studied the reports but never found signs of beings from other planets. Most scientists do not believe in UFOs. But they do believe in the need to study and enjoy the solar system—and our place in it.

INDEX